ABOUT:

The book covers a wide range of topics that are essential for anyone looking to go fishing in Europe. The section on types of fishing available in Europe, such as freshwater fishing, saltwater fishing, and fly fishing, provides a great overview of the different options and helps readers determine which type of fishing is best for them. The section on essential fishing gear for European fishing is also very useful, as it provides detailed information on rods and reels, lines and leaders, baits and lures, hooks and sinkers, and other gear that is needed for successful fishing.

The book also provides an in-depth look at popular fishing destinations in Europe, including freshwater fishing destinations like rivers, lakes, and streams, and saltwater fishing destinations like the Mediterranean, Atlantic, and North Sea. It provides detailed descriptions of the types of fish found in these bodies of water, as well as techniques for catching them. The section on fly fishing in Europe is particularly comprehensive and provides a great introduction to this popular and challenging form of fishing.

The book also covers important regulations and con servation concerns in European fishing, including catch lim its and size restrictions, protected species and habitats, lic ensing and permit requirements, and other important rules and regulations. This section is crucial for ensuring that fis hing in Europe is sustainable and responsible, and it helps readers understand their responsibilities as anglers.

Finally, the book concludes with a section on planni ng your European fishing trip. This section provides practic al advice on choosing a fishing destination, selecting the ri ght time of year to go fishing, arranging transportation and accommodation, and planning a budget for your fishing tri p. Overall, this book is a comprehensive and valuable reso urce for anyone interested in fishing in Europe. Whether y ou are a seasoned angler or a beginner, this book will help you make the most of your fishing experience in Europe.

TABLE OF CONTENTS

Chapter 1: Introduction to European Fishing

Chapter 2: Essential Fishing Gear

Rods and reels

Lines and leaders

Baits and lures

Hooks and sinkers

Chapter 3: Freshwater Fishing in Europe

Overview of freshwater fishing in Europe

Types of fish found in European freshwater bodies

Techniques for freshwater fishing

Chapter 4: Saltwater Fishing in Europe

Overview of saltwater fishing in Europe

Popular saltwater fishing destinations (e.g. Mediterranean, Atlantic, North Sea)

Types of fish found in European saltwater bodies

Techniques for saltwater fishing

Chapter 5: Fly Fishing in Europe

Overview of fly fishing in Europe

Popular fly fishing destinations (e.g. rivers, streams)

Types of fish that can be caught using fly fishing (e.g. trout , grayling, salmon)

Essential gear for fly fishing (e.g. fly rods, reels, flies)

Techniques for fly fishing (e.g. dry fly fishing, nymph fishin g, streamer fishing)

Chapter 6: Spin Fishing

Chapter 7: Baitcasting Fishing in Europe

Chapter 8: Float Fishing

Chapter 9: Regulations and Conservation in European Fishing

Overview of fishing regulations in Europe

Catch limits and size restrictions, protected species and h abitats, licensing and permit requirements

Chapter 10: Planning Your European Fishing Trip

Choosing a fishing destination

Selecting the right time of year to go fishing

Arranging transportation and accommodation

Planning a budget for your fishing trip

Chapter 11: Conclusion

This book provides comprehensive information on fi shing in Europe, including gear and techniques, popular fis hing destinations, regulations and conservation, and plann ing a fishing trip. Whether you are a seasoned angler or a beginner, this book will help you make the most of your fis hing experience in Europe.

CHAPTER1

Overview of fishing in Europe

Fishing is a beloved pastime and sport enjoyed by millions of people around the world, and Europe is no exception. With its diverse landscapes, rich history, and abundant waterways, fishing in Europe is a unique and rewarding experience that appeals to anglers of all levels.

Europe is home to numerous freshwater and saltwater fishing destinations, each offering its own unique opportunities to catch a variety of fish species. From the majestic rivers of the Alps to the tranquil lakes of Scandinavia and the rugged coastline of the Atlantic, European fishing destinations are as varied as the fish themselves.

Freshwater fishing is a popular activity in Europe, and the continent boasts some of the world's most famous trout streams, salmon rivers, and carp lakes. Whether you prefer spinning, baitcasting, or fly fishing, Europe has plenty of opportunities to put your angling skills to the test.

Saltwater fishing is also an important part of Europe's fishi ng heritage. The Mediterranean, Atlantic, and North Sea are home to a diverse array of saltwater fish species, inclu ding cod, mackerel, pollock, and more. Whether you prefer trolling, jigging, or bottom fishing, saltwater fishing in Europe provides a unique and exciting angling experience.

Fly fishing is a specialized type of fishing that is becoming increasingly popular in Europe. With its clear, cold streams and rivers, Europe is home to some of the world's finest fly fishing destinations, offering the chance to catch trout, grayling, and salmon. Fly fishing requires special gear an d techniques, and the experience of casting a fly and feeli ng the pull of a fish is a unique and rewarding one.

In addition to its diverse fishing opportunities, Europe is also known for its rich fishing culture and history. From the Nordic tradition of fly fishing for salmon to the medieval art of angling in England, fishing has been a part of Europe's cultural heritage for centuries. Whether you are interested in the history of fishing or simply looking for a unique angling experience, fishing in Europe is a must-try for any fishing enthusiast.

In conclusion, fishing in Europe is a unique and rewarding experience that offers something for anglers of all levels. From its diverse fishing destinations to its rich history and culture, fishing in Europe provides an unforgettable experience that is sure to leave a lasting impression on all who take part.

Popular fishing destinations in Europe

Europe is home to numerous stunning fishing destinations offering a wide variety of fishing experiences for anglers of all levels. From the stunning scenery to the rich marine life, Europe is a paradise for fishing enthusiasts. Here are some of the most popular fishing destinations in Europe:

- Norway: Known for its picturesque fjords, crystal clear waters and diverse fish species, Norway is a top

destination for fishing enthusiasts. The country's co
astline is dotted with numerous fishing villages, pro
viding easy access to the best fishing spots.
Salmon, cod, halibut, and mackerel are some of the
most popular catches in Norway.

- Scotland: Scotland's west coast is renowned for its
abundant sea life and stunning scenery, making it a
top destination for fishing. The country's waters are
home to a wide range of fish species, including
salmon, sea trout, and haddock. Many of Scotland's
fishing villages offer guided fishing trips and accom
modation for those who want to make a holiday out
of it.

- Ireland: Ireland is famous for its wild and rugged
coastlines and stunning scenery, making it a top de
stination for fishing. The country's rich marine life is
home to a wide range of fish species, including sal
mon, sea trout, and haddock. There are also numer
ous rivers and lakes in Ireland, providing ample opp
ortunities for freshwater fishing.

- Iceland: Iceland is known for its stunning glaciers,
rugged coastline, and abundant fish life, making it a

top destination for fishing. The country's waters are home to a wide range of fish species, including cod , haddock, and halibut. Many fishing villages in Icel and offer guided fishing trips and accommodation fo r those who want to make a holiday out of it.

- France: France is renowned for its rich culture, stunning scenery, and diverse fishing opportunities. From the Atlantic coast to the Mediterranean, France offers a wide range of fishing experiences fo r anglers of all levels. The country's waters are hom e to a wide range of fish species, including salmon, sea trout, and haddock.

In conclusion, Europe is a paradise for fishing enthusiasts, offering a wide variety of fishing experiences and stunning scenery. Whether you are an   experienced angler or just starting out, you are sure to find a fishing destinatio n in Europe that suits your needs.

Types of fishing available in Europe (e.g. freshwater fishin g, saltwater fishing, fly fishing

Europe offers a wide variety of fishing experiences for anglers of all levels, with a range of different fishing metho ds available. Here are some of the most popular types of fishing available in Europe:

- Freshwater Fishing: Europe is home to numerous rivers, lakes, and streams, providing ample opportu nities for freshwater fishing. From the stunning mou ntain lakes of Switzerland to the rolling hills of Scotl and, Europe's freshwater fishing destinations offer a peaceful and scenic environment for anglers. Fres hwater fishing in Europe typically involves catching species such as trout, pike, and carp.
- Saltwater Fishing: Europe's coastline is dotted with numerous fishing villages and ports, providing easy access to the best saltwater fishing spots. From the rugged coastlines of Ireland to the crystal clear wat ers of Norway, Europe's saltwater fishing destinatio ns offer a diverse range of fishing experiences.

Saltwater fishing in Europe typically involves catching species such as cod, mackerel, and salmon.

- Fly Fishing: Europe is home to some of the best fly fishing destinations in the world, offering a unique and challenging experience for anglers. From the rolling hills of Scotland to the pristine rivers of Sweden, Europe's fly fishing destinations offer a peaceful and scenic environment for those looking to test their skills. Fly fishing in Europe typically involves catching species such as trout, grayling, and salmon.

In conclusion, Europe offers a wide range of fishing experiences for anglers of all levels, with a range of different fishing methods available. Whether you are interested in freshwater fishing, saltwater fishing, or fly fishing, you are sure to find a fishing destination in Europe that suits your needs.

Foto ilustrates winter fishing.

Chapter 2: Essential Fishing Gear for Europe an Fishing

Rods and reels

Fishing in Europe offers a wide variety of experiences for anglers of all levels, from freshwater streams to saltwater ports. To make the most of your fishin g trip, it is essential to have the right gear. In this essay, we will focus on two of the most important pieces of fishing gear: rods and reels.

Rods: The right rod can make a huge difference in your fishing experience. When fishing in Europe, you should choose a rod that is appropriate for the type of fishi ng you will be doing. For example, if you are going to be fly   fishing, you will need a lightweight and flexible rod that can handle the delicate presentations required for this method. On the other hand, if you are going to be saltwat er fishing, you will need a heavier and stiffer rod that can handle the strong currents and powerful fish species found in these waters.

Reels: A good fishing reel is also essential for a successful fishing trip in Europe. When choosing a reel, you should consider the type of fishing you will be doing and the speci es you will be targeting. For example, a reel with a good drag system is important for saltwater fishing, where you may need to fight powerful fish species such as cod or mackerel. For fly fishing, you may want to choose a reel with a large spool that can hold a sufficient amount of line, allowing you to make longer casts.

In conclusion, having the right rods and reels is essential to a successful fishing trip in Europe. When choosing gear , consider the type of fishing you will be doing, the species you will be targeting, and the conditions you will be facing. With the right gear, you can ensure that you have a fun and productive fishing experience in Europe.

Lines and leaders

Lines and leaders are two other important pieces of fishing gear that are essential for a successful fishing trip i n Europe. Here is more information about these items:

Lines: The line you choose can greatly impact your fishing experience. For example, if you are fly fishing, you will need a lightweight and delicate line that allows you to make delicate presentations. For saltwater fishing, you may want to choose a heavier and more durable line that can handle strong currents and powerful fish species. There are many different types of fishing lines available, including monofilament, fluorocarbon, and braided lines, each with its own benefits and drawbacks.

Leaders: Leaders are used to connect the line to the hook and are especially important when fishing in clear water where visibility is high. Leaders help to reduce the visibility of the line, making it less likely that the fish will be spooked. The size and strength of the leader will depend on the type of fishing you will be doing and the species you will be targeting.

In conclusion, having the right lines and leaders can greatly impact your fishing experience in Europe. When choosing lines and leaders, consider the type of fishing yo u will be doing, the species you will be targeting, and the conditions you will be facing. With the right gear, you can ensure that you have a fun and productive fishing experience in Europe.

Baits and lures

The most common used baits for fishing in Europe vary depending on the type of fishing and the species being targeted. However, some of the most popular baits used include:

- Live baits: Live baits, such as worms, maggots, or minnows, are often used when fishing for species such as carp, pike, or perch in freshwater.
- Artificial lures: Artificial lures, such as crankbaits, spinnerbaits, or soft plastics, are often used when fishing for species such as bass, trout, or sea bream in freshwater or saltwater.
- Cut baits: Cut baits, such as mackerel or squid, are often used when fishing for species such as cod, pollock, or dogfish in saltwater.
- Squid or octopus: Squid or octopus is a common bait used when fishing for species such as cod, haddock, or whiting in saltwater.

It is important to note that the most effective bait for a particular species and location can vary and may depend on many factors, such as season, weather and water conditions. Anglers should also familiarize themselves with local fishing regulations regarding the use of live and artificial baits.

Hooks and sinkers

Hooks and sinkers are two essential pieces of fishing gear that are crucial for a successful fishing trip in Europe. Here is more information about these items:

- Hooks: Hooks are used to secure the bait or lure to the line and are one of the most important pieces of fishing gear. The type of hook you choose will depend on the species you are targeting and the type of fishing you will be doing. For example, if you are fishing for smaller species, such as trout or perch, you may choose a smaller hook, while for larger species, such as cod or sea bass, you may choose a larger hook.
- Sinkers: Sinkers are used to control the depth at which your bait or lure will be fished and are especially important when fishing in deeper water. There are many different types of sinkers available, including split shot sinkers, egg sinkers, and bank sinkers, each with their own benefits and drawbacks.

Chapter 3: Freshwater Fishing in Europe

Overview of freshwater fishing in Europe

Freshwater fishing in Europe offers a diverse and exciting experience for anglers of all skill levels. From the clear and pristine mountain streams of the Alpine regions to the wide and winding rivers of the lowlands, Europe is home to some of the world's best freshwater fishing destinations. Here is an overview of freshwater fishing in Europe:

- Species: Europe is home to a wide variety of freshwater fish species, including trout, pike, carp, catfish, perch, and many others. Each species has its own unique characteristics, habits, and preferred habitats, which can greatly impact your fishing experience.
- Techniques: There are many different techniques used in freshwater fishing, including fly fishing, spin

fishing, bait casting, and others. The technique you choose will depend on the species you are targeting, the type of water you will be fishing in, and your personal preferences.

- Regulations: Freshwater fishing in Europe is regulated by local, regional, and national authorities , and it is important to familiarize yourself with these regulations before fishing. Regulations may include restrictions on fishing methods, the use of live baits , and catch limits.

- Tackle: The type of tackle you will need for freshwater fishing in Europe will depend on the species you are targeting, the type of water you will be fishing in, and the technique you will be using. Common pieces of tackle include rods, reels, lines, hooks, baits, and lures.

- Destinations: Europe is home to many fantastic freshwater fishing destinations, including Lake Geneva in Switzerland, the River Ebro in Spain, the River Rhine in Germany, and the River Severn in the UK, to name just a few.

In conclusion, freshwater fishing in Europe offers an exciting and diverse experience for anglers of all skill level s. With a wide variety of species, techniques, regulations, tackle, and destinations, there is something for everyone in this wonderful region. Whether you are a seasoned angler or a beginner,   Europe is the perfect place to enjoy the sport of freshwater fishing.

Popular freshwater fishing destinations (e.g. rivers, lakes, streams)

Europe is home to many fantastic freshwater fishing destinations, each offering its own unique challenges and opportunities for anglers. Here are some of the most popular freshwater fishing destinations in Europe:

- Lake Geneva, Switzerland: Lake Geneva is a large and beautiful lake that is home to a wide variety of freshwater fish species, including trout, pike, perch, and others. The lake is surrounded by stunning mountain scenery and is a popular destination for anglers from around the world.

- River Ebro, Spain: The River Ebro is one of Spain's largest rivers and is a popular destination for freshwater fishing. The river is known for its large catfish, as well as its carp, pike, and other species.

- River Rhine, Germany: The River Rhine is one of Europe's largest and most important rivers, and is a popular destination for freshwater fishing. The river is home to a wide variety of species, including trout, pike, and perch, and is also known for its excellent fly fishing opportunities.

- River Severn, UK: The River Severn is the longest river in the UK and is a popular destination for freshwater fishing. The river is known for its large and abundant stocks of salmon, as well as its trout, pike, and other species.

- Alpine streams, Austria and Switzerland: The Alpine regions of Austria and Switzerland are home to many pristine mountain streams and rivers that offer fantastic freshwater fishing opportunities. These strea ms are known for their clear waters, abundant trout populations, and stunning mountain scenery.

- River Danube, Germany and Austria: The River Danube is one of Europe's largest rivers and is a popular destination for freshwater fishing. The river is home to a wide variety of species, including carp, catfish, pike, and others.
- River Loire, France: The River Loire is the longest river in France and is a popular destination for fresh water fishing. The river is known for its excellent carp fishing, as well as its pike, perch, and other species.
- River Po, Italy: The River Po is Italy's largest river and is a popular destination for freshwater fishing. The river is home to a wide variety of species, including catfish, carp, and others.
- Lake Como, Italy: Lake Como is a large and beautiful lake in Italy that is known for its excellent freshwater fishing. The lake is home to a wide

variety of species, including trout, perch, and pike, and is surrounded by stunning mountain scenery.

- River Vltava, Czech Republic: The River Vltava is the longest river in the Czech Republic and is a popular destination for freshwater fishing. The river is known for its abundant stocks of trout, as well as its pike, perch, and other species.

- River Shannon, Ireland
- Lake Balaton, Hungary
- River Tees, UK
- River Avon, UK
- River Oder, Germany
- River Meuse, Belgium
- River Tisza, Hungary
- Lake Zürich, Switzerland
- River Elbe, Germany
- Lake Plitvice, Croatia
- River Trent, UK
- River Clyde, Scotland
- River Arno, Italy

- River Aare, Switzerland
- Lake Garda, Italy
- River Weser, Germany
- Lake Constance, Germany and Switzerland
- River Guadiana, Spain
- River Dordogne, France
- River Dniester, Ukraine and Moldova
- River Volga, Russia
- River Sava, Slovenia and Croatia
- River Save, Serbia and Bosnia-Herzegovina
- River Theiss, Hungary

- These are just a few of the many freshwater fishing destinations available in Europe. Each one offers unique fishing opportunities, as well as stunning natural beauty, making them popular destinations for anglers from around the world.

Types of fish found in European freshwater bodies

- Trout: Trout are a popular gamefish in Europe and are found in many rivers, lakes, and streams. There are several species of trout found in Europe, including brown trout, rainbow trout, and brook trout.
- Carp: Carp are one of the most widely-distributed fish species in Europe and are commonly found in rivers, lakes, and reservoirs. They are a popular target for anglers and are known for their size and strength.
- Bass: Bass are a popular sportfish in Europe and are found in many lakes, rivers, and estuaries. There are several species of bass found in Europe, including largemouth bass, smallmouth bass, and spotted bass.
- Catfish: Catfish are a common species found in European rivers, lakes, and reservoirs. They are known for their size and fighting spirit and are a popular target for anglers.

- Pike: Pike are a predatory fish found in many European rivers, lakes, and streams. They are a popular gamefish for anglers and are known for their strength and agility.
- Perch: Perch are a common species found in European freshwater bodies and are a popular target for anglers. They are known for their vibrant coloration and are considered a prized catch by many   anglers.
- Zander: Zander, also known as pike-perch, is a species of fish found in European rivers, lakes, and streams. They are a popular gamefish for anglers and are known for their size and fighting spirit.
- Chub: Chub are a common species found in European rivers, lakes, and streams. They are a popular target for anglers and are known for their fighting spirit and excellent taste.
- Roach: Roach are a common species found in European freshwater bodies and are a popular target for anglers. They are known for their abundant populations and are considered a staple species by many anglers.

- Barbel: Barbel are a species of fish found in Europe an rivers and are known for their strong fighting spirit and delicious taste.
- Tench: Tench are a species of fish found in Europe an lakes, ponds, and rivers and are known for their size and fighting spirit.
- Eel: Eel are a species of fish found in European rivers, lakes, and estuaries. They are known for their elusive nature and are considered a prize catch by many anglers.
- Bullhead: Bullhead are a species of fish found in European rivers, streams, and ponds. They are known for their hard-fighting nature and are a popular target for anglers.
- Bream: Bream are a common species found in European rivers, lakes, and estuaries. They are known for their size and delicious taste and are a popular target for anglers.
- Grayling: Grayling are a species of fish found in European rivers, lakes, and streams. They are

known for their beauty and fighting spirit and are a popular target for anglers.

- Salmon: Salmon are a species of fish found in European rivers and are known for their size and strength. They are a popular gamefish for anglers and are sought after for their quality as a table fish.
- Rudd: Rudd are a species of fish found in European rivers, lakes, and ponds. They are known for their abundant populations and are a popular target for anglers.
- Wels Catfish: Wels Catfish are a species of fish found in European rivers, lakes, and reservoirs. They are known for their size and fighting spirit and are a popular target for anglers.
- Rainbow trout: Rainbow trout are a species of fish found in European rivers and streams. They are prized for their beauty and fighting spirit and are a popular target for fly fishing.
- Brown trout: Brown trout are a species of fish found in European rivers and streams. They are known for their size and strength and are a popular target for anglers.

- Arctic char: Arctic char are a species of fish found in some European rivers and lakes in northern regions. They are prized for their delicious taste and are a popular target for anglers.
- Brook trout: Brook trout are a species of fish found in European streams and rivers. They are known for their beauty and fighting spirit and are a popular target for anglers.
- Arctic grayling: Arctic grayling are a species of fish found in some European rivers in northern regions. They are prized for their beauty and are a popular target for fly fishing.

These are just a few of the many types of fish that can be found in European freshwater bodies. The variety and diversity of species in Europe make it an exciting and rewarding place to fish.

Freshwater fishing in Europe offers a wide range of techniques and styles, each with its own unique set of challenges and rewards. Some of the most   popular techniques for freshwater fishing in Europe include:

- Spin fishing: Spin fishing is a popular technique for fishing in European rivers and lakes. It involves using a spinning rod and reel to cast a lure or bait and retrieve it back to the angler.
- Baitcasting: Baitcasting is a popular technique for fishing in European rivers and lakes. It involves using a baitcasting rod and reel to cast a bait or lure and retrieve it back to the angler.
- Fly fishing: Fly fishing is a popular technique for fishing in European rivers and streams. It involves using a fly rod and reel to cast a fly, which is designed to imitate an insect or other food source, to a target fish.
- Float fishing: Float fishing is a popular technique for fishing in European rivers and canals. It involves

using a float to suspend a bait or lure at a specific depth, attracting fish to bite.

- Bottom fishing: Bottom fishing is a popular technique for fishing in European lakes and ponds. It involves fishing near the bottom of the water body, using a bait or lure to attract fish.

- Trolling: Trolling is a popular technique for fishing in European lakes and rivers. It involves using a boat to tow one or more fishing lines, with lures or baits, behind the boat to attract fish.
- Jigging: Jigging is a popular technique for fishing in European lakes and rivers. It involves using a jig, which is a type of bait or lure with a weighted head and a soft body, to imitate a swimming or jumping prey, attracting fish to bite.
- Spincast fishing: Spincast fishing is a hybrid technique that combines elements of spin fishing and baitcasting. It involves using a spincast rod and reel to cast a lure or bait, providing an easy-to-use

option for beginners or anglers looking for a more relaxed fishing experience.

- Nymph fishing: Nymph fishing is a type of fly fishing that focuses on fishing with artificial flies designed to imitate the aquatic insects that fish feed on. It is a popular technique for fishing in European rivers and streams and requires a specialized set of skills and gear.

- Dry fly fishing: Dry fly fishing is a type of fly fishing that focuses on fishing with artificial flies that float on the water surface. It is a popular technique for fishing in European rivers and streams and requires a specialized set of skills and gear.

These are just a few of the many techniques for freshwater fishing in Europe, each offering a unique set of challenges and rewards. Whether you prefer using a spinning rod, fly rod, or any other type of gear, there is a freshwater fishing technique that will suit your needs and interests.

Overview of saltwater fishing in Europe

- Saltwater fishing in Europe is a popular activity along the coasts of the Mediterranean, the North Sea, and the Atlantic Ocean. With an abundance of saltwater species, including mackerel, cod, sea bass, and more, anglers have plenty of opportunities to catch trophy fish in European waters.

- In saltwater fishing, anglers use a variety of techniques, including trolling, bottom fishing, casting, and jigging, to target different species of fish. Trolling is a popular technique for fishing in European waters, as it allows anglers to cover a large area and target a variety of species. Bottom fishing is also popular, as it offers the opportunity to target larger species, such as cod and sea bass, that dwell near the sea floor.

- In addition to traditional techniques, saltwater fishing in Europe also offers the opportunity to catch large game fish, such as marlin and tuna, through sportfishing. These species can be caught using heavy tackle and specialized techniques, providing an exciting challenge for experienced anglers.

- Whether you are a seasoned angler or a beginner, saltwater fishing in Europe offers something for everyone. From the crystal-clear waters of the Mediterranean to the rough seas of the North Atlantic, there are plenty of opportunities to catch fish and enjoy the great outdoors.

Popular saltwater fishing destinations

- Mediterranean Sea: The Mediterranean is one of the most popular saltwater fishing destinations in Europe, known for its warm, crystal-clear waters and diverse marine life. The Mediterranean is home to species such as bluefin tuna, swordfish, and dorado, and is a popular destination for sportfishing

- Atlantic Ocean: The Atlantic Ocean provides a wealth of fishing opportunities for anglers along the European coast, from the waters of Scotland to the beaches of Portugal. The Atlantic is home to species such as cod, halibut, mackerel, and sea bass, and is a popular destination for both sportfishing and commercial fishing.

- North Sea: The North Sea is a rough and challenging fishing ground that is home to species such as cod, plaice, and herring. The North Sea is a popular destination for commercial fishing, as well as for anglers looking for a more rugged and challenging fishing experience.

- Bay of Biscay: The Bay of Biscay is located on the western coast of France and is known for its rich fishing grounds and diverse marine life. The Bay is home to species such as bluefin tuna, cod, and sea bass, and is a popular destination for sportfishing.
- The English Channel: The English Channel is located between England and France and is known for its rich fishing grounds and diverse marine life. The Channel is home to species such as plaice, cod, and sea bass, and is a popular destination for both sportfishing and commercial fishing.

These are just a few of the many popular saltwater fishing destinations in Europe, each offering a unique set of fishing opportunities and challenges. Whether you prefer the warm waters of the Mediterranean or the rough seas of the North Atlantic, there is a saltwater fishing destination in Europe that will suit your needs and interests.

Types of fish found in European saltwater bodies

- Cod: Cod is one of the most popular fish species in Europe, found in the cold waters of the North Sea and the Atlantic Ocean. Cod is a popular target for both commercial and sport fishing, and is known for its delicate, flaky white flesh.
- Mackerel: Mackerel is a fast-swimming species that is found in the waters of the Atlantic Ocean, from the shores of Portugal to the coast of Scotland. Mackerel is a popular target for sport fishing, and is known for its oily, flavorful flesh.
- Pollock: Pollock is a groundfish species that is found in the waters of the North Atlantic and is a popular target for commercial fishing. Pollock is known for its mild, white flesh and is used in a variety of dishes, including fish and chips.
- Tuna: Tuna is a warm-water species that is found in the waters of the Mediterranean and the Atlantic Ocean. Tuna is a popular target for sport fishing, and is known for its meaty, flavorful flesh.

- Sardines: Sardines are small, oily fish species that are found in the waters of the Mediterranean and the Atlantic Ocean. Sardines are a popular target for commercial fishing, and are used in a variety of dishes, including sardine pâté and sardine fillets.
- Sea Bass: Sea Bass is a predatory species that is found in the waters of the Mediterranean and the Atlantic Ocean. Sea Bass is a popular target for sport fishing, and is known for its delicate, flavorful flesh.

These are just a few of the many fish species that can be found in the saltwater bodies of Europe, each offering its own unique set of challenges and rewards for anglers.

*Techniques for saltwater fishing (e.g. bottom fishing, trollin
g, jigging*

- Bottom Fishing: Bottom fishing involves fishing near
  the bottom of the ocean, using heavy weights to
  keep the bait or lure in place. This technique is
  often used to target species such as cod, haddock,
  and flounder.
- Trolling: Trolling involves pulling a fishing line
  behind a moving boat, using lures or baits to attract
  fish. Trolling is often used to target pelagic species
  such as tuna, mackerel, and wahoo.
- Jigging: Jigging involves using a specialized fishing
  lure that is designed to mimic the movements of a
  baitfish. Jigging is often used to target species such
  as cod, pollock, and haddock in deep waters.
- Spinning: Spinning involves using a spinning reel
  and rod to cast and retrieve lures or baits. Spinning
  is a versatile technique that can be used in both
  freshwater and saltwater, and is often used to

target species such as sea trout, sea bass, and mackerel.

- Baitcasting: Baitcasting involves using a specialized reel and rod to cast heavy baits or lures. Baitcasting is often used to target larger species such as tuna, marlin, and shark.

Overview of fly fishing in Europe

Fly fishing is a popular and exciting form of fishing that is enjoyed by anglers all over the world, including in Europe. Fly fishing involves casting a lightweight, artificial fly that imitates the appearance and behavior of various insects, to entice fish to bite.

One of the great things about fly fishing is that it can be done in a variety of freshwater environments, including rivers, streams, and lakes. Some of the most popular fly fishing destinations in Europe include the rivers and streams of Scotland, Wales, and Ireland, where wild brown and rainbow trout can be caught. Other popular destinations include the chalk streams of England, which are famous for their large populations of trout, grayling, and even salmon.

The essential gear for fly fishing includes a fly rod, reel, line, leader, and a selection of flies. The fly rod and reel are designed to be lightweight and easy to cast, with the rod length and action being selected based on the type of fishing being done. Flies are typically tied using feathers, fur, and other materials, and can range in size from tiny midge patterns to large streamers.

There are many different techniques used in fly fishing, each designed to mimic a different type of insect or food source. Some of the most common techniques include:

- Dry Fly Fishing: Dry fly fishing involves casting a floating fly that is designed to imitate adult insects that are either hatching or resting on the surface of the water.
- Nymph Fishing: Nymph fishing involves fishing a subsurface fly that is designed to imitate the immature stages of various insects.
- Streamer Fishing: Streamer fishing involves fishing a large, streamer-style fly that is designed to imitate small baitfish or other aquatic prey.

Fly fishing is a great way to experience the beauty and tranquility of Europe's freshwater environments while pursuing the thrill of the catch. Whether you are an experienced angler or a beginner, fly fishing is a fun and rewarding way to spend time on the water.

Chapter 6: Spin Fishing

Spin fishing, also known as spin casting, is a popular and versatile type of fishing that is widely enjoyed by anglers in Europe. Spin fishing involves using a spinning rod and reel to cast a lure or bait that is designed to imitate a variety of different prey species.

One of the great things about spin fishing is that it can be done in a variety of freshwater and saltwater environments, making it a popular choice for anglers of all experience levels. In Europe, some of the most popular spin fishing destinations include the rivers, lakes, and streams of the UK and Ireland, as well as the many coastal areas of the Mediterranean and Atlantic.

The essential gear for spin fishing includes a spinning rod, reel, line, and a variety of lures or baits. The spinning rod and reel are designed to be lightweight and easy to cast, with the length and action of the rod being selected based on the type of fishing being done. Lures and baits can range in size from tiny jigs to large crankbaits, and are typically designed to imitate various types of prey such as worms, minnows, and other small fish.

There are many different techniques used in spin fishing, each designed to target different species of fish. Some of the most common techniques include:

- Spin Casting: Spin casting involves casting a lure or bait and reeling it back in slowly, using a steady retrieve. This technique is often used to target species such as bass, pike, and perch.
- Trolling: Trolling involves pulling a lure or bait behind a moving boat, using a slow and steady retrieve. This technique is often used to target species such as salmon, trout, and mackerel.
- Jigging: Jigging involves casting a heavy jig and then rapidly lifting and dropping it to create a lifelike swimming action. This technique is often used to target species such as cod, pollock, and other bottom-dwelling species.

In addition to these techniques, spin fishing can also be done using a variety of different lures and baits, each designed to imitate a specific type of prey. For example, soft plastic worms are often used to imitate worms or other small creatures, while crankbaits are designed to imitate small fish or other prey species.

Spin fishing is a great way to experience the beauty and excitement of Europe's freshwater and saltwater environments while pursuing the thrill of the catch. Whether you are an experienced angler or a beginner, spin fishing is a fun and rewarding way to spend time on the water. With its versatility and ease of use, spin fishing is a popular choice for anglers of all experience levels and is sure to provide you with many unforgettable fishing experiences.

Chapter 7: Baitcasting Fishing in Europe

Baitcasting Fishing in Europe: An Overview

Baitcasting fishing is a popular method of fishing in Europe, and itAs an effective way to catch fish in both freshwater and saltwater environments. The technique involves using a baitcasting rod and reel combination that allows the angler to cast with precision and accuracy, making it a great choice for both novice and experienced fishermen.

Popular Baitcasting Fishing Destinations in Europe

There are many popular baitcasting fishing destinations in Europe, including rivers, lakes, and even coastal regions. Some of the most popular locations include the River Seine in France, the River Rhine in Germany, and the River Po in Italy. These destinations offer an excellent opportunity to catch a variety of fish species, including catfish, pike, and even bass.

Types of Fish that Can be Caught with Baitcasting

Baitcasting is an effective method for catching a variety of fish species in Europe, including both freshwater and saltwater fish. In freshwater bodies such as rivers, lakes, and streams, anglers can target species like catfish, pike, and bass. In saltwater environments, species like cod, mackerel, and pollock are often caught using baitcasting techniques.

Essential Gear for Baitcasting Fishing

In order to successfully catch fish with baitcasting, you will need to invest in the right gear. This includes a high-quality baitcasting rod, reel, and line. Some anglers also prefer to use specialized lures and baits, such as crankbaits, jigs, and spinnerbaits. Additionally, its important to have a comfortable and sturdy fishing chair, as well as a well-stocked tackle box with all of the necessary hooks, sinkers, and other gear.

Techniques for Baitcasting Fishing

There are several techniques that are commonly used when baitcasting, including spin fishing, trolling, and jigging. Spin fishing is one of the most popular techniques, and it involves using a spinning reel with a light action rod. The angler casts the bait out into the water and then retrieves it in a slow, steady motion, allowing the fish to bite.

Trolling is another popular baitcasting technique, and it involves pulling a lure or bait behind a boat while it moves through the water. This method is often used to target larger saltwater species, such as mackerel and pollock.

Jigging is a popular technique for catching fish in deeper water, and it involves using a heavy jig with a hook attached to it. The angler drops the jig to the bottom of the body of water, and then jigs it up and down, allowing the fish to bite.

In conclusion, baitcasting is a popular method of fishing in Europe, and it offers anglers the opportunity to catch a variety of fish species in both freshwater and saltwater environments. With the right gear, techniques, and patience, anyone can enjoy a successful day of baitcasting fishing.

Chapter 8: Float Fishing in Europe

Float fishing is a popular and versatile angling method in Europe. It is used to catch a variety of fish species in both freshwater and saltwater bodies, including rivers, lakes, streams, and the sea. The technique involves suspending a bait at a specific depth below a floating device, which serves to indicate a bite and to help keep the line vertical. This allows anglers to target different species of fish at different depths, making it a great all-round fishing method.

Overview of Float Fishing in Europe

Float fishing has been a popular angling method in Europe for many years, with roots that can be traced back to ancient times. The technique involves using a floating device, often referred to as a float, to suspend a bait at a specific depth in the water. The float can be made of different materials, including cork, balsa wood, or plastic, and is typically brightly coloured to make it easier to see in the water.

The float serves two main purposes. Firstly, it provides visual indication of a bite, as the float will dip or disappear when a fish takes the bait. Secondly, it helps to keep the line vertical, which is essential for presenting the bait in the correct manner to the fish.

Popular Float Fishing Destinations in Europe

There are many popular float fishing destinations throughout Europe, with each offering its own unique angling opportunities. Some of the most popular destinations include:

- River Seine, France - The River Seine is one of the most popular float fishing destinations in France, offering a wide range of species for anglers to target.
- Lake Garda, Italy - Lake Garda is one of the largest and most beautiful lakes in Europe, and is a great

destination for float fishing. It is well-known for its a
bundant stocks of trout, carp, and catfish.

- River Rhine, Germany - The River Rhine is one of
  the longest and most important waterways in
  Europe, and is a popular float fishing destination for
  anglers.
- River Po, Italy - The River Po is one of the longest
  rivers in Italy, and is a popular destination for float
  fishing. It is known for its large populations of carp,
  catfish, and perch.

Types of Fish that can be Caught with Float Fishing in
Europe

Float fishing is a versatile technique that can be used to
catch a wide variety of fish species in both freshwater and
saltwater environments. Some of the most common
species caught using float fishing in Europe include:

- Carp - Carp are one of the most popular target
  species for float fishing in Europe, and are found in
  many rivers, lakes, and streams throughout the
  region.

- Trout - Trout are widely distributed throughout Europe, and are a popular target species for float fishing. They are often caught in rivers, streams, and lakes.
- Catfish - Catfish are found in many European rivers and canals, and are often caught using float fishing. They are known for their powerful fighting ability and can provide a challenging and rewarding experience for anglers.
- Perch - Perch are a widespread and abundant species in Europe, and are often caught using float fishing. They are known for their aggressive feeding habits, making them a popular target species for anglers.

Essential Gear for Float Fishing in Europe:

- Rods: Float fishing rods are usually between 7-10 feet in length and are designed for light to medium action fishing. They are typically made of graphite or fiberglass and come in a range of power and tapers to suit different fishing styles.

- Reels: Baitcasting reels are the preferred choice for float fishing, as they provide the angler with the necessary control and line retrieval speed needed to successfully catch fish. A good baitcasting reel should be smooth and durable, with a strong drag system.
- Lines: Monofilament fishing line is the most common choice for float fishing, as it provides good sensitivity and casting performance. However, fluorocarbon line can also be used for float fishing, especially when fishing in clear water, as it has a lower visibility and higher sensitivity.
- Floats: Floats are a key component in float fishing and come in a variety of shapes, sizes, and materials. A float's purpose is to suspend the bait at a specific depth and to serve as a visual indicator of a bite.
- Hooks: Float fishing hooks come in a range of sizes and shapes and should match the type of bait being used. The size of the hook should be appropriate for the size of the fish being targeted and the type of fishing being done.

- Sinkers: Sinkers are used to control the depth at which the bait is fished and to help keep the line tight. The size and type of sinker will depend on the depth being fished, the type of bait being used, and the type of fishing being done.
- Baits: Live bait, such as worms, maggots, or minnows, is often used for float fishing. Artificial baits, such as soft plastics or jigs, can also be used. The type of bait being used will depend on the type of fishing being done, the type of fish being targeted, and the time of year.

In addition to these essential pieces of gear, float fishing also requires some basic fishing skills, including the ability to cast accurately, control the float, and set the hook when a fish bites. Float fishing is a great way to enjoy the outdoors and target a variety of fish species, including carp, catfish, and panfish.

Chapter 9: Regulations and Conservation

Overview of fishing regulations in Europe

Fishing regulations in Europe vary greatly depending on the country and region, but the overarching aim is to conserve and protect the natural aquatic habitats and species. The regulations typically include measures such as:

- License requirements: Many European countries require a fishing license for both freshwater and saltwater fishing. This license may be required for both residents and non-residents, and can be obtained from the local fishing authority or from a local tackle shop.
- Catch and release: To protect fish stocks and conserve the fishing environment, many European countries encourage anglers to practice catch and

release, particularly for certain species of fish. This means returning the fish back to the water unharmed after it has been caught.

- Size and bag limits: Many European countries have size and bag limits in place, which determine the minimum and maximum size of fish that can be caught, as well as the number of fish that can be taken per day. This helps to conserve the fish populations and maintain sustainable fishing practices.
- Seasonal restrictions: Certain species of fish may only be caught during specific times of the year, and fishing may be restricted during the breeding or spawning season.
- Bait and tackle restrictions: The use of certain types of bait and tackle may be restricted in some European countries, particularly to protect sensitive aquatic habitats and endangered species.
- Fishing methods: Certain fishing methods, such as gill netting, may be banned in some European countries to protect the aquatic habitat and its inhabitants.

It is important for anglers to familiarize themselves with the fishing regulations in the region they plan to fish in, as failure to follow these regulations can result in significant fines and legal penalties. By following these regulations, anglers can help to ensure that the fishing resources in Europe are conserved and protected for generations to come.

Catch limits and size restrictions protected species and ha bitats, licensing and permit requirements

Fishing regulations in Europe vary from country to country, but most have established catch limits and size restriction s to conserve fish populations and maintain the health of aquatic ecosystems.

Catch limits refer to the maximum amount of a particular s pecies of fish that can be taken by a single angler in a give n period of time, often a day or a week. The purpose of cat ch limits is to prevent overfishing and ensure that fish pop ulations remain sustainable.

Size restrictions, on the other hand, specify the minimum size that a fish must be in order to be legally harvested. This is to protect young and immature fish that have not yet had a chance to reproduce and contribute to the population's survival.

Both catch limits and size restrictions help to maintain healthy fish populations and ensure that future generations of anglers will have the opportunity to enjoy the sport of fishing.

It is important for anglers to familiarize themselves with the fishing regulations in the areas they plan to fish and to always follow the rules to help protect the fish and their habitats.

In addition to catch limits and size restrictions, fishing regulations in Europe also protect certain species and habitats. Some species, such as certain types of salmon, may be designated as "protected" and have additional restrictions on the times they can be caught and the methods that can be used.

Habitats can also be protected to ensure that they are not disturbed by fishing activities. This can include sensitive areas such as spawning grounds, migratory routes, and areas that support important food sources for fish.

Licensing and permit requirements are also common in European fishing regulations. These requirements ensure that only those who have completed necessary training and follow the rules are allowed to fish in a particular area. Permits may be required for access to certain waters or for fishing certain species.

It is important for anglers to obtain the proper licenses and permits before fishing in any given area, and to familiarize themselves with the regulations and restrictions that apply . This not only helps to protect the fish and their habitats, but also ensures that anglers are fishing legally and responsibly.

Chapter 10: Planning

Fishing   Trip

Europe offers a wealth of fishing opportunities, with a wide variety of freshwater and saltwater bodies, as well as abundant species of fish. Whether you're an experienced angler or a beginner, a well-planned fishing trip can be an enjoyable and memorable experience. Here are some key considerations when planning your European fishing trip.

Choosing a Fishing Destination

The first step in planning your fishing trip is to choose a destination that meets your needs and interests. Consider factors such as the type of fishing you want to do (e.g. freshwater, saltwater, fly fishing), the type of fish you want to target (e.g. trout, bass, cod), and the level of difficulty you're comfortable with. Research popular fishing destinations in Europe to find the best options for your trip.

Selecting the Right Time of Year to Go Fishing

The timing of your trip can greatly impact your fishing experience. Some species of fish are only available during certain times of the year, so you'll need to research the best time to target your desired species. In addition, the weather and water conditions can vary greatly through out the year, so it's important to consider the impact of these factors on your fishing experience.

Arranging Transportation and Accommodation

Once you've selected your fishing destination, you'll need to arrange transportation and accommodation. Consider factors such as proximity to the fishing locations, comfort and amenities, and cost when choosing your accommodations. You may also need to consider the availability of rental equipment, guides, and other fishing-related services.

Planning a Budget for Your Fishing Trip

Fishing trips can range from simple, low-cost excursions to elaborate and expensive adventures. Before you start planning your trip, it's important to have a clear understanding of your budget. Consider the cost of transportation, accommodation, fishing gear and licenses, as well as any other expenses such as food, drink, and souvenirs. Plan your trip accordingly and allocate your budget in a way that maximizes your enjoyment of the fishing experience.

In conclusion, planning your European fishing trip requires careful consideration of many factors, including the type of fishing you want to do, the timing of your trip, the cost of transportation and accommodation, and your budget. With proper planning and preparation, you can ensure that your fishing trip is a success and a memorable experience.

Chapter 11: Conclusion

In conclusion, fishing in Europe offers a rich and diverse experience, with a variety of freshwater and saltwater destinations, an abundance of different types of fish, and a range of techniques and gear to choose from. From the famous rivers and lakes, to the stunning coastlines and seas, Europe is home to some of the world's best fishing spots. The region's rich history and culture are also evident in its fishing traditions and practices, making it a truly unique and unforgettable experience. Whether you're an experienced angler or a beginner, fishing in Europe is a must-try for all anglers looking for a new and exciting challenge. With careful planning and preparation, you can make your fishing trip in Europe an unforgettable and rewarding experience.

Printed in Great Britain
by Amazon